Pitch What's
True

A Publisher's Tools for Navigating
Your Best Path to a Published Nonfiction Book

{ a workbook }

Sharon Woodhouse

Everything Goes Media
Chicago • Milwaukee
www.everythinggoesmedia.com

Pitch What's True: A Publisher's Tools for Navigating Your Best Path to a Published Nonfiction Book

by Sharon Woodhouse

ISBN: 978-1-893121-60-7
LCCN: 2018966091

Published April 2019 by:

Everything Goes Media, LLC
www.everythinggoesmedia.com

Many thanks to Stacey Lane Smith for proofreading the final product and for her excellent editorial suggestions along the way.

Printed in the United States of America

23 22 21 20 19   10 9 8 7 6 5 4 3 2 1

Contents

1. Preface 1
2. Start on the Road to Publishing with Proper Smarts 3
3. . . . Then Add Flair 6
4. A Word on This New Relationship 8
5. A Quick Note about Agents, Self-Publishing, and Hybrid Publishing.. 13
6. Savvy Author Checklist 14
   - Do You Have General Publishing Knowledge? 15
   - Do You Have Knowledge of the Specific Publisher You're Pitching? 23
   - The Book.. 299
   - The Author 355
   - Sales & Marketing 455
7. Proposal Summary.. 53
8. Cheat Sheet: Find the Right Publisher for Your Nonfiction Book 566
9. Conclusion 66
10. Master Checklist of the Benefits of Being an Author 677
11. About the Author.. 70
12. More 71
    - Amazon Reviews 71
    - Future Books and Classes................................. 71
    - Coaching.. 71

Skin in the game is robust,
soul in the game is antifragile.*

---

* Nassim Nicholas Taleb, *Antifragile: Things That Gain from Disorder* (New York: Random House, 2012).

Preface

10,000. In the twenty-five years I've been publishing books, while running my own publishing companies and publishing consultancy, that's how many queries[1], pitches[2], proposals, manuscripts, and submissions I estimate I've heard, read, skimmed, reviewed, or evaluated. Ten thousand pitches do not equal the 10,000 hours to mastery of Malcolm Gladwell's theory[3] (from *Outliers: The Story of Success*), but I'm going to say it's close.

The material in this book was created and refined over the last twenty years. It has been presented in workshops to thousands of writers and authors-to-be.

But it's not simply the accumulated knowledge of an expert. **The Book, The Author,** and **Sales & Marketing** checklists contained in this book are the actual assessment tools that my editorial team and I use in-house when evaluating possible projects. Nor is this book simply a peek inside the mind of a publisher.

---

[1] By queries I mean both inquiries in general as well as that keystone of the publishing process, the *query letter*—a one-page missive (two pages only if you simply can't help it) to an agent or publisher outlining your book project and inquiring after the reader's potential interest in it.
[2] Pitch here is even more generic; it's any and all manner of proposal lobbed at someone in publishing with decision-making clout.
[3] The theory has since been debunked anyway.

My contribution is just the savvy and solid foundation from which *you* will be launching *your* nonfiction book project. Through the workbook component of *Pitch What's True*, you will be bringing forth the real value of your nonfiction content and creating a winning proposal to put in front of publishers. You will be consciously considering the best of you and your book, what you truly have to offer, what the world actually needs, and real ways for your book to reap economic and additional benefits for yourself and others.

In doing the work within—sincerely, creatively, and thoughtfully—you will emerge with a well-crafted, well-considered proposition. The right publisher will want to be your partner in bringing your book to the world.[4]

—Sharon Woodhouse

---

[4] I hope that upon finishing this book, many of you will realize that in light of today's publishing landscape and its opportunities *you* or *you working with a hybrid publisher* may be the best publisher for your work.

Start on the Road to Publishing with Proper Smarts . . .

Over the last several years, I've seen umpteen lines in print about how authors and writers in our digital age are making less money than ever. Reporters quoting writers declare it, "barely a sustenance-level living!" One high-profile author and spokesperson even pronounced writers "endangered." Others have, in all somber seriousness, noted that writing what others need, want, and/or are willing to pay for is one way writers may be able to make a living at their craft.

If you're writing high-quality, useful, provocative, inspiring, educational, fill-in-your-own-estimable-adjective nonfiction that meets needs or wants, then don't entangle yourself in those worries and debates. You have something to offer the marketplace and something to contribute to the world. This book exists to put you on the path to be remunerated for that.

Consider: people are still hungry for knowledge and entertainment, and most people are too Google-brained to communicate effectively through the written word. You know what I'm talking about. Maybe the world is becoming less dependent on the written word. That's a big maybe. Nonetheless, it is certain that good writing, which never came easily to most people, is becoming harder than ever, even for those whom it used to be easy. If you can write well, that's sufficiently rare and that alone makes it valuable.

Beyond financial reward, I hope this book expands your picture of what publishing your book and becoming an author can be and what that can mean for your life. Writing a book good enough for a publisher to agree to invest their limited time, money, and energy on can open up a world of new possibilities for you...both if you *let* that happen (i.e., no self-sabotage) and if you help *make* that happen.

In publishing dozens of authors and in assisting an even greater number of consulting clients, I have seen countless times over the last two decades how an author can accrue a whole package of personal benefits when he or she approaches the entire publishing process seriously, realistically, and holistically. Start smart. Do it right from the beginning—before you get the contract[5]—and keep going on that route once you do.

My **Savvy Author Checklist** focusing on The Book, The Author, and Sales & Marketing, followed by the **Proposal Summary, Cheat Sheet for Finding the Right Publisher for Your Nonfiction Book,** and **Master Checklist of the Benefits of Being an Author** are short (enough) and simple (in their way), but well-honed and full of hard-earned knowledge. Please use these tools, my experience, and my insights to make your publishing journey as easy, delightful, and fruitful as possible.

---

[5] Really, this should be: before you write a word. Getting the publishing process off on the right foot means getting the writing started with the end result in mind.

To that end, I've added exercises to this material[6] to make it a workbook, to force your hand a little further and increase the odds that you'll dig deep, cover your bases, and do the best job possible on your nonfiction book proposal.

Let's get started on pitching what's true.

---

[6] Much of this book's contents began as a handout that accompanied a "How to Pitch Yourself As (and Really Be) a Savvy Nonfiction Author" program I gave for years. It later appeared as the ebook *10,000 Pitches: Savvy Nonfiction Book Proposals: A Publisher Shares Her Checklists, How-To's, and Fundamental Notions for Approaching Publishers with Your Ideas.*

. . . Then Add Flair

Following the advice in this document is no guarantee that you will find an ideal publisher for your book and secure the publishing contract and experiences of your dreams. But I do guarantee that the information that follows will give you a very strong start for navigating in the world of *traditional* publishing[7] to the best of your ability. Let's face it. Not only has publishing always been a bit of a private club, seemingly mysterious and closed to outsiders—and even elitist and labyrinthine—it lately has been in perpetual disruption mode to boot.

Once you grasp the material spelled out in this workbook and how it applies to your project, proceed with confidence in preparing your queries and proposals. Feel free to then add your personal style to the mix. Approach it methodically. Persevere, revise, and polish as you go. It's your best shot.

If you do not find the right publisher for you in a reasonable amount of time (as determined by you), you will have a solid grounding in the business and a perspective from

---

[7] Traditional publishing refers to the type of book publishing traditionally practiced by the established book publishing industry. Publishers offer authors contracts in which they essentially buy or borrow the publishing rights from the author. The publisher then manages the publishing process and accepts responsibility for all publishing costs, paying authors a share of sales revenues as royalties.

which you can evaluate your remaining options (for example, self-publishing[8] or hybrid publishing[9]) and move on.

At a minimum, add flair. Soul is better.[10]

---

[8] Self-publishing is book publishing overseen and financed by the author without the involvement of an established publishing company.

[9] Hybrid publishing refers to all mash-ups of self-publishing and traditional publishing, and it is increasingly becoming the norm for many small and independent publishers. The IBPA (Independent Book Publishers Association) has published a list of quality and ethics guidelines for hybrid publishers that I highly recommend anyone pursuing a hybrid route understand thoroughly and take to heart before entering into such a business arrangement (www.ipba-online.org/page/hybridpublisher).

[10] See epigraph.

A Word on This New Relationship

A business relationship is a relationship. Finding a publisher is the beginning of establishing a long-term business *relationship*. Keep that forefront in your mind, as well as everything you know about positive, healthy, mutually beneficial relationships, as you continue through the process.

Know that you are bringing something specific and valuable to the table...and so are the publishers. Do they want what you're offering? Do you want what they're offering? What sort of relationship are you looking for here, and how can you do your share to create that as you go?

Respect yourself, respect your book, and respect the publisher/s. Nurturing high-quality connections and partnerships as you go about this process is one of the keys to publishing success—and one of its rewards as well.

I may have mentioned *relationship* a few times. Before we get started on my lists: *what specific and valuable things are you bringing to a publisher? Consider any and all aspects of your content, you as a person, and the economic and other opportunities you bring as a package. This is just early dreaming and brainstorming. Refinement and reality can come later!*

❏ _____

❏ _____

❑ _____
❑ _____
❑ _____
❑ _____
❑ _____
❑ _____
❑ _____
❑ _____

And what are the things you want from a publisher?

❑ _____
❑ _____
❑ _____
❑ _____
❑ _____
❑ _____
❑ _____
❑ _____
❑ _____
❑ _____

How would you describe your ideal author-publisher relationship?

_____
_____
_____
_____
_____
_____
_____

_____

_____

_____

What are some of your best relationship skills? What are some ways they can help you as you proceed?

_____

_____

_____

_____

_____

_____

_____

_____

_____

_____

_____

What are some of your weaker relationship skills? What are some ways you can bolster those, compensate for them, or work around them?

_____

_____

_____

_____

_____

_____

_____

_____
_____
_____
_____

What does respecting yourself and your book through this process look like to you?

_____
_____
_____
_____
_____
_____
_____
_____
_____
_____

How will you respect the publishers with whom you come into contact?

_____
_____
_____
_____
_____
_____
_____
_____
_____

If at this point, you are already disinclined to do the exercises, guess what? You don't have to do them! You can pick and choose which ones to do. You can skim for the main ideas and skip any real thinking. You can chuck the reading and dip in only as a reference. You can stick this book in the next Little Free Library you pass.

But consider this: studies show that one of the best predictors of whether or not you will behave optimally (as you most desire, in service of your end goal, as your best self, etc.) in some future situation is simply if you have previously thought about how you would act or be in that situation.

"The harder I work, the luckier I get."

—Samuel Goldwyn

"Fortune favors the prepared mind."

—Louis Pasteur

So prepare yourself. Do your research. Think through the details. Clarify your aims. Walk yourself through future scenarios. Know what's true now and what you want to be true down the road. Just do the work.

A Quick Note about Agents, Self-Publishing, and Hybrid Publishing

While this content is specifically for nonfiction authors who want to directly pitch and submit their projects to publishers, it is also useful for those seeking an agent.[11] Adjust accordingly. It can also be immensely handy for those who plan to self-publish or enter hybrid publishing arrangements. If you will be your own publisher, have you considered everything you need to? Consult the **Savvy Author Checklist**, and view your project from an external perspective. How does it rate? How can it be improved to increase its odds of success?

---

[11] For online advice on agents, turn to the cache of articles on and by literary agents at WritersDigest.com or the one-stop shop of MarkMalatesta.com. Former literary agent Mark Malatesta also manages the free database of literary agents at www.literaryagencies.com (you need to provide an email address and sign in for access). If you have a book that you think—know—could go big, you want an agent if you can get one. Spend at least 2–4 months contacting 1–5 agents a day with your best possible efforts before pursuing other options. Publishing is a numbers game, often a big numbers game. Work the numbers.

Savvy Author Checklist

And so here it goes. Before, during, and after the preparation of your queries, pitches, proposals, and/or manuscript submissions to publishers, use the following to make sure you've covered all the bases.

Do You Have General Publishing Knowledge?

☐ Do you understand the publisher's perspective (in general)?

☐ Do you understand how the publishing industry works?

☐ Do you understand industry norms?

☐ Do you understand what's typically and realistically expected of authors?

☐ Do you understand how the publishing industry is changing and how that affects publishers?

As far as all of the above goes, where are your knowledge gaps when it comes to publishing? What do you still need to know or better understand?

_____

_____

_____

_____

_____

_____

_____

_____

_____

_____

_____

_____

_____

_____

_____

_____

_____

Here's a reminder: Just Google it! Look at what you've written above, and consider Googling for your answers. Some suggested inputs: How does traditional book publishing work? What do publishers expect of authors? How do publishers choose the books they publish? What is typical in the book publishing industry? What are the latest trends in book publishing?

☐ Do you know what your publishing options are, including self-publishing, digital publishing,[12] hybrid publishing, and even...not publishing!?

A few research notes on self-publishing:

_____
_____
_____
_____
_____
_____
_____
_____
_____
_____
_____
_____

A few research notes on digital publishing:

_____
_____
_____
_____
_____

---

[12] A broad, vague term that's applied to publishing online and/or in a range of electronic formats.

_____

_____

_____

_____

_____

_____

_____

_____

_____

_____

A few research notes on hybrid publishing:

_____

_____

_____

_____

_____

_____

_____

_____

_____

_____

_____

_____

_____

_____

Is it possible that you shouldn't put in the effort to publish? Is _not_ publishing an option for you? What are some other options for your content, material, and knowledge besides putting it in a book? What are some other options for your life besides going down any publishing path?

_____

_____

_____
_____
_____
_____
_____
_____
_____
_____
_____
_____
_____
_____
_____

☐ Have you used reference materials found at public libraries such as _Literary Marketplace_ and _Publishers Marketplace_ to increase your knowledge?

If not, when will you go to the library to do this?

_____
_____

Once you've done this, what are some of the most important and surprising things you learned? What do you want to remember for future use?

_____
_____
_____
_____
_____
_____
_____
_____
_____

_____

_____

☐ Have you used print/online magazines, such as *Writer's Digest,* to increase your knowledge?

If not, when will you do this?

_____

_____

Once you've done this, take note of some of your discoveries to keep in mind for down the road.

_____

_____

_____

_____

_____

_____

_____

_____

_____

_____

_____

_____

_____

☐ Have you used online resources—websites, writer's forums (LinkedIn groups and others), blogs, e-newsletters, and social media—to increase your knowledge?

If not, when will you do this?

_____

_____

Which sites do you need to return to for further study?

_____

_____

_____

_____

_____

_____

_____

_____

_____

_____

As you explore these sites, jot down those things you want to remember about the publishing industry.

_____

_____

_____

_____

_____

_____

_____

_____

_____

_____

_____

_____

☐ Have you joined writer/author groups in your area to share knowledge and connect with others?

If not, when will you do research on local groups?

_____

_____

Once you've done this, list the groups you'd like to test out in person.

_____

_____

_____
_____
_____
_____
_____

As you go about connecting with and learning from others in your region, make some notes for yourself.

_____
_____
_____
_____
_____
_____
_____
_____
_____
_____
_____
_____
_____
_____
_____
_____

☐ Have you attended lectures, presentations, classes, or workshops by publishers or about publishing to gain the knowledge you need?

If not, when will you do research on the options available to you?

_____
_____

Once you've done some research, note the opportunities you'll explore here (and add them to your calendar now).

_____
_____
_____
_____
_____
_____
_____
_____

As you learn from experts, keep a list of their best pieces of advice and other relevant information.

_____
_____
_____
_____
_____
_____
_____
_____
_____
_____
_____
_____
_____
_____
_____
_____
_____

Do You Have Knowledge of the Specific Publisher You're Pitching?

☐ What is the publishing mission and/or vision of the company you're approaching?

Make notes on elements of a company's mission and/or vision that could potentially be a good fit for you and your book. (You may want to start a separate notebook so that you have enough room to answer the questions below for multiple publishers.)

_____

_____

_____

_____

_____

_____

_____

_____

_____

_____

☐ Is your book a good fit for the company in terms of subject? Approach? Philosophy? Format?

What is your book's subject?

_____

_____

_____

_____

_____

_____

_____

Approach?

_____

_____

_____
_____
_____
_____
_____
_____

Philosophy?

_____
_____
_____
_____
_____
_____

Format?

_____
_____
_____
_____
_____
_____

☐ Does it fit with any of their current or forthcoming books? Will it fill any holes in their backlist[13]?

Imagine where your book meshes with and distinguishes itself from others within a particular niche or genre.

_____
_____
_____
_____

---

[13] A publisher's backlist is the collection older titles a company still has in stock, available for sale (as opposed to a year's new releases...the "frontlist").

_____
_____
_____
_____
_____
_____

☐ Will your book open up new groups of customers for this particular publisher or help them build on their existing customer base?

Who are the different types of readers and customers[14] for your book?

_____
_____
_____
_____
_____
_____
_____
_____
_____

☐ What are the strengths and weaknesses of this publisher, and how does your book fit within that structure?

Consider what kind of strengths or weaknesses a publishing company could have that could work (or not work) in you and your book's favor.

_____
_____
_____
_____

[14] Readers read books. Customers buy books. Customers include individuals, libraries, schools, bookstores, gift shops, wholesalers, clubs, organizations, corporations, etc.

_____
_____
_____
_____
_____
_____
_____

☐ How has this publisher done with books similar to yours? With authors similar to you? How well have these books sold, and by what means have they sold?

What kinds of authors and books will you be on the lookout for on possible publishers' front and backlists?

_____
_____
_____
_____
_____
_____
_____
_____
_____
_____
_____

☐ Who are this publisher's customers? Does your book meet their needs, likes, and level of knowledge?

What are the needs, likes, and level of knowledge of likely readers and customers of your book?

_____
_____
_____
_____
_____

_____
_____
_____
_____
_____
_____
_____

☐ Are there new developments related to this publisher's area(s) of specialty that they are likely to want to address, develop, or exploit?

What changes in your own field, advances in your book's subject areas, and local/global trends should be promoted to a publisher so that together you, they, and your book can capitalize on them?

_____
_____
_____
_____
_____
_____
_____
_____
_____
_____
_____

☐ Is the publisher releasing ebooks[15]? Developing mobile apps? Are they current and savvy when it comes to new

---

[15] A book released in any digital format, such as a .pub, .mobi (for the Amazon Kindle), or .pdf file.

technologies and online and non-traditional methods of promotion?

What nonprint formats and technologies do you see as relevant, promising, or necessary for your material?

_____

_____

_____

_____

_____

_____

_____

_____

_____

☐ What does this publisher expect of its authors in working relationships? Editorial involvement? Marketing and promotion?

What sort of publisher expectations will throw up a red flag for you? Is anything a deal breaker? In what areas do you have boundaries that you won't cross in your negotiations?

_____

_____

_____

_____

_____

_____

_____

_____

_____

_____

_____

Know that publishers will be looking at...

The Book

Your book as a print and/or digital product.

☐ Does your book meet the highest standards in terms of content? Style? Mechanics?

If not, in which areas does it fall short? Who or what can help you raise your manuscript to a level of excellence? How and when will you correct those things?

_____

_____

_____

_____

_____

_____

_____

_____

_____

_____

☐ Does your book deserve to exist? Does it deserve the publisher's investment of time, expertise, and funding? Does it deserve readers' time in a busy world?

So...does it? What makes your book worthy of attention and expenditure...by a publisher? By readers? By stores with limited shelf space? What makes allotting time to read your book preferable to Netflix, yoga, drinking with friends, playing with kids, or a few extra hours of work or sleep?

_____

_____

_____
_____
_____
_____
_____
_____
_____

☐ Is there an audience for your book with an important,
    unfilled need?

Who are they?

_____
_____
_____
_____
_____
_____
_____

What is their need?

_____
_____
_____
_____
_____
_____
_____

*How does your content meet that need and to what
extent?*

_____
_____
_____

_____
_____
_____
_____
_____

Should your material be adapted in light of these answers?

_____
_____
_____
_____
_____
_____
_____

☐ Does your book cover its topic for the first time or for the first time in a particular way or from a particular angle? Does your book take us a step forward in thinking about a particular subject?

What is your book's particular subject, and what are its points of distinction? How do you break new ground and add originality or perspective?

_____
_____
_____
_____
_____
_____
_____
_____
_____

☐ Do your voice, approach, and/or style draw the reader to your material and make it irresistible or somehow fresh and unique?

If so, how? How would you describe these advantages to a publisher? If not, what changes need to be incorporated to make it so? Will you need help with that? What kind of help?

_____
_____
_____
_____
_____
_____
_____
_____
_____
_____

☐ Is there a mass or targeted audience large enough to support your book?

*We will look at reaching your audience in greater depth in the **Sales & Marketing** section, but for now, contemplate this from a justification point of view. Are there enough people who will benefit from and want to read your book? Moreover, will you and the publisher be able to reach them easily and economically enough to warrant the entire bundle of resources you'd have to devote to that end?*

_____
_____
_____
_____
_____

☐ Will your book be financially feasible for the publisher in terms of the amount of editing/development/production/marketing work and expense required? Can the publisher produce and price your book competitively?

The specifics of any publisher's expenses and financial reckonings are unavailable to you, but engage your commonsense and intuition. Using what you know from bookstore pricing, can the book you're proposing be priced so that its natural audience will readily buy it? Are you submitting a package of written (and where relevant graphical) material that will not incur undue costs to transform into a book?

☐ How is your book conceived as a package[16]? Is it complete in content and approach? Will it include photos, maps, sidebars, a bibliography, notes, etc.? Are there gaps in content coverage? Photo coverage? Is your book's category obvious at first glance?

Can you conceive of your book as a package? If not, what considerations will help you get there? If so, what elements of your book as a package need tweaking or enhancement?

_____

_____

_____

_____

_____

_____

_____

_____

_____

_____

☐ Does it lend itself to non-print formats/technologies?

Which ones? How might these extend the book's reach?

_____

_____

_____

_____

_____

_____

_____

_____

---

[16] Just letting you know that I use "package" here, in no formal capacity, to mean the whole kit and caboodle, your book in its conceptual entirety.

Publishers will be closely examining...

The Author

You as a writer, a thought leader, a promoter, and a promotable figure.

☐ Have you done your best in writing your book in terms of content, style, and mechanics? Is your best good enough?

What are your book's weaknesses in this area? Who can give you objective feedback? If you can't get impartial assessments from friends, family, or fellow writers, who can you hire for this job? When will you address this?

_____
_____
_____
_____
_____
_____
_____
_____
_____

☐ What are your overall credentials and the general experience level conveyed by your résumé? Are you qualified to write this book? Have you been published before? Where?

Answer the above questions for yourself. How do you feel about your overall qualifications? Which will you emphasize when interacting with potential publishers? Are there any obvious deficits you'll need to account for?

_____
_____

_____
_____
_____
_____
_____
_____
_____
_____
_____
_____
_____

☐ Are your credentials appropriate for your topic...and obvious to those who care? Are you credible? Knowledgeable? An expert? Hobbyist? Insider? Does it matter for your topic?

Answer these questions below, and then re-read your answers as if you are a publisher. What sense do you get of author-topic fit? Where do you shine? Do you have any new insights that will help with your proposal?

_____
_____
_____
_____
_____
_____
_____
_____
_____
_____
_____

☐ Are you passionate about your work and your subject? Will you ever get tired of it? Can you sustain a high level of enthusiasm for and devotion to it?

Can you answer these questions with a resounding Yes!? If not, what do you need to get there? Are you sure this is the right subject for you? What are some ways you might be able to sustain a fitting level of commitment to your book over time?

_____

_____

_____

_____

_____

_____

_____

_____

_____

_____

☐ Are you a professional? Do you approach your work and the publishing process professionally? Will you treat the publisher's staff respectfully?

Considering the above questions, make some notes for yourself on what to keep in mind going forward.

_____

_____

_____

_____

_____

_____

_____

_____

_____

_____

☐ Are you appropriately attentive to details, deadlines, commitments, and pre-[17] and post-production[18] responsibilities?

How will you fit these things into the life you already have? What things will have to change to make it all possible?

_____

_____

_____

_____

_____

_____

_____

_____

_____

_____

_____

☐ Do you have an awareness of what those details, commitments, and responsibilities are?

If not, how can you find out what you need to know?

_____

_____

_____

_____

_____

_____

[17] Pre-production refers to what happens before a book's production work (editing, design, indexing, and the like), such things as writing, re-writing, contract negotiations, and getting to know the publisher's people.
[18] Post-production refers to what happens after the book's production work is complete, usually starting the minute the book goes to press (i.e., it's at the printing company being printed...almost no publisher owns their own printing presses), primarily meaning sales and marketing activities.

_____

_____

_____

_____

_____

☐ Will you be easy to work with as an author? Are you honest? Reliable? Personable? Can the publisher trust you with their reputation? To represent them? Will they be proud to have published you?

What are your best relationship and business skills, and how can you enlist those talents on behalf of your book? In what ways will publishing you enhance a publisher's reputation?

_____

_____

_____

_____

_____

_____

_____

_____

_____

☐ Will you be easily accessible to the publisher? The media? The public?

How responsive are you currently to those who call you on the phone or email you? Will your current level of responsiveness bring the results you want when it comes to replying to a publisher, the media, and the public (your readers)? Do you need to adjust your thinking and your behaviors to increase your response rate, polish your communication, and/or up your customer service?

_____
_____
_____
_____
_____
_____
_____
_____
_____
_____
_____
_____

☐ What is your degree of interest, willingness, ability, and availability to market your book? Do you have media experience? Are you willing to learn? Can you speak comfortably, engagingly, and authoritatively on your subject?

Answer the above. Where do you feel strong? Where do you feel less confident? You will need to market your book and interact with the media at some point. How can you get started in this area? With what strengths will you lead? What skills are you willing to learn? What workarounds can you devise for impediments you foresee?

_____
_____
_____
_____
_____
_____
_____
_____

_____

_____

_____

_____

☐ Do you have the connections (how many?) to promote a book and the skills/interest necessary to mine those connections? Do you have Facebook, LinkedIn, Twitter, and/or other active social media accounts and a system for always increasing your connections there?

Do you? Make a list of everyone you know. Everyone. Personally and professionally. Get out your address book and your holiday card list. Add your email contacts, your phone contacts, and your Facebook friends. Consider the extent of their networks. Consider the reach of your current social media accounts. Do you need to start or become more active on any social media platforms? Are there one or two that suit you and your audience that you can focus on? What are ways you can systematically increase your connections over time?

_____

_____

_____

_____

_____

_____

_____

_____

_____

_____

_____

_____

_____

_____

_____

☐ Do you have an email list? An e-newsletter? A website? A blog? A column? A syndicated column? A speaking career? What are the ways you currently reach out to others with your message(s)? What ways are you developing or willing to develop?

Answer these questions (without panicking!). If you have any of the above, do they need enhancing to accommodate your book and book promotion activities? In what ways? When will you do those things? If not, which ones make sense for your purposes? How and when will you bring those things into being, and how will you maintain and develop them?

_____

_____

_____

_____

_____

_____

_____

_____

_____

_____

_____

_____

_____

_____

_____

_____

☐ How does your online presence already fit with your future as an author, your book(s), and your topic(s)? How do you plan to adjust if you need to? Are you actively participating online in current conversations relevant to your topic(s) in as many forums as make sense?

What jumps out in answering these questions? What modifications can you make? Where are your customers and readers online? What subject area conversations can you meaningfully contribute to?

_____
_____
_____
_____
_____
_____
_____
_____
_____
_____
_____
_____
_____
_____
_____
_____
_____

☐ Are you aware of the amount of work, stamina, and new skills, and the different outlook required to properly promote a book?

If not, who can give you a realistic perspective? When will you contact them for specifics and advice? How and when will you clear your schedule to make all of the above possible? Who can you enlist for support and accountability?

_____
_____
_____
_____
_____

☐ Are you, as an individual, promotable? Do you have a personality (or persona) that makes you particularly saleable and appealing?

What are your most endearing, inspiring, and intriguing features? What are some ways you can put these characteristics front and center on behalf of your book?

And publishers give at least equal, if not greater, consideration to...

Sales & Marketing

Opportunities for you, the publisher, your fans, and other vested parties to promote and sell the book.

☐ Will your book sell? Why? Does your book have competition? How many other books are in the market on this subject? On tangential subjects? Does your book meet the competition in value and content?

So...will your book sell? Why? What makes it better or different than competitive titles? What are the strengths and weaknesses of those titles, and how does your book fit within that space?

_____

_____

_____

_____

_____

_____

_____

_____

_____

_____

_____

_____

_____

_____

☐ What is your book's story? Its human interest features? What makes your book an "event" or a "thing?" The subject? The author? The approach? Its timeliness? Its relation to current events? Its celebration or evolution of its subject?

What is your book's story? What are its primary points of appeal?

_____

_____

_____

_____

_____

_____

_____

_____

_____

_____

_____

_____

☐ Does your book have a strong enough hook? Is its "story" significant enough, appealing enough, complex enough, and rich enough for continual promotion? What will prompt readers to talk about the book?

How can you take advantage of your book's points of appeal? Do any of these elements need amplification? What changes to your manuscript or your approach can be made to strengthen this important aspect of marketing?

_____

_____

_____

_____

_____

_____
_____
_____
_____
_____
_____
_____
_____
_____

☐ Is this book easy and appealing for bookstores, libraries, gift shops, avid readers, thought leaders, bloggers, Tweeters, and anyone with a social media account, a mobile device, or a mouth to talk about, promote, and stand behind? Why?

Time to brainstorm. List all the easy and obvious talking points that others should readily be sharing about your book.

_____
_____
_____
_____
_____
_____
_____
_____
_____
_____
_____
_____
_____

☐ Are there enough different angles for constant promotions? For creative marketing? What is the degree of interest, loyalty, and passion for the subject among likely readers?

Back at it...what <u>other</u> angles are there? What are <u>all</u> the facets that expected fans might appreciate about what you have? How many different ways can you engage likely readers?

☐ Can the publisher reach the natural audience for your book efficiently, easily, affordably, and through new online media and retailers? Through their current distribution channels? Through new channels that are easy to forge? Through new channels that they would like to develop? Through new channels that would also benefit at least some of their other titles?

What might you know about your audience that a publisher wouldn't? What information about this crowd can you share? What else do they read? Where do they shop? What are their other interests? Who do they talk to about this topic and where? What do they talk, think, and care about? How can this information open up new opportunities for a publisher?

_____
_____
_____
_____
_____
_____
_____
_____
_____
_____
_____
_____
_____
_____
_____

☐ Does your book have potential in other formats (audio, video, children's, foreign language, ebook, database, subscription website, mobile app, etc.)?

Which ones? What makes your content a good fit for these other formats? How can your content be adapted or enhanced? How easily?

_____
_____
_____
_____
_____
_____
_____
_____
_____
_____
_____

_____

_____

☐ What are the opportunities to sell primary[19] or secondary[20] rights for your book (e.g., excerpts, TV, film, book club, and multimedia)?

Answer the question. Then jot down some notes on what makes your book's content right for those situations. Next, what about the "how"—how might those sales take place—and the "who"—who might realistically purchase such rights?

_____

_____

_____

_____

_____

_____

_____

_____

_____

_____

_____

_____

_____

_____

[19] Primary rights typically refer to any rights a publisher secures (most contracts will secure them all) that they may pursue (or desire to prevent others from pursuing) directly. These may include the rights to publish hardcovers, paperbacks, mass market paperbacks, ebooks, audiobooks, mobile apps, multimedia versions, etc.

[20] Secondary (or subsidiary rights) are the class of rights (also procured in nearly every contract) that are normally not exploited by a publisher but sold or licensed, if possible, to other parties. These may include film, theater, and television rights; commercial and merchandising rights; and foreign translations. A publishing contract spells out the publisher/author revenue split if any of these rights are sold.

_____

_____

☐ Does your book have a reasonably long—or indefinite—shelf life? Will it fare well on the backlist? Will it require minimal updating, or will it be easy enough to update when necessary?

How long? Why? If your book endures, how often should it be updated, and what will that entail? How will you keep current on your topic and revise your book as needed?

_____

_____

_____

_____

_____

_____

_____

_____

_____

_____

_____

☐ Does your book lend itself to cross-promotions with other titles the company publishes? What multiple book/author events and synergies are possible? Will your book lead readers to other titles the company publishes?

Return to this question for every customized pitch you make to a publisher. List some beginning ideas in this area to get you started thinking along these lines.

_____

_____

_____

_____

☐ What nontraditional channels are open to this book? What type of bulk sales opportunities exist for this book?

Brainstorm on both below. Where beyond bookstores and libraries can this book be sold? What sort of people and organizations might purchase multiple copies of this book at once? For what purpose? Who needs 10 books? 100 books? 1,000 books?

In short...

→ Do you have something (a fleshed-out idea/book concept, partial manuscript, finished manuscript, or complete package) you believe (better yet, *know*) to be of real value? If so, continue. If not, go back to that first and alter as needed. What are the missing or weak links? Can/should this current project be salvaged and reworked so that it *is* of real value, or should it be set aside in favor of your next and better idea?

Just be honest. Is your offering ready to be out there? You're aiming for <u>real value</u> and not perfection. If not, what do you need to do next?

_____
_____
_____
_____
_____
_____
_____
_____
_____
_____
_____

→ Combine what you now know about the publisher's perspective in general and each particular company* with what they want to know about you (*see* **The Book, The Author**, and **Sales & Marketing** above) and put real effort and *flair* into your most persuasive proposal package.

Do you have the big picture in sight? What is the flair, polish, and personality you can bring, and how are you infusing that into your proposition?

_____

_____

_____

_____

_____

_____

_____

_____

→ * Yes, tweak each proposal package/pitch appropriately for every single publisher. You and your proposal(s) will be appreciably more effective when the recipient feels they're reading something freshly and thoughtfully prepared just for them. Think about it.

This doesn't have to be onerous. Where are the obvious places in your package that you can customize the pitch for each publisher? Make some notes on the language you'll use for those points.

_____

_____

_____

_____

_____

_____

_____

_____

→ Review the tone and content of your proposal package. Remove anything overwrought, inflated, exaggerated, needy, irrelevant, or over-explained.

What needs refinement or has to be cut?

_____

_____

_____

_____

_____

_____

_____

_____

→ If (that's a critical *if!*) you have something of value, believe it deeply and act calmly and confidently from that place. Know it, own it, and approach the publisher as an equal, looking to enter into a mutually beneficial business relationship. Adjust your attitude and mindset to this setting before you begin the journey. Then put in the mental effort to keep it there.

Do you have it? Can you own it? Are you there? If not, what do you need to get there? Get to that place, get the help you need, and get going.

_____

_____

_____

_____

_____

_____

_____

_____

_____

Cheat Sheet: Find the Right Publisher
for Your Nonfiction Book

Here's my overall, one-size-fits-most, best approach to locating a publisher that's a terrific match for you and your project, if (1) you're not self-publishing or (2) your book is not a likely candidate for one of the big New York publishing houses (meaning an agent is much less likely to take it on). Among the remaining 10,000 small to mid-sized publishers or remaining 80,000[21] micro-publishers[22] in the U.S., there may be a handful of houses ready to make you an offer.

☐ Spend a few hours on Amazon researching existing books on your topic and any topic, really, that is aimed at your book's likely audience. Take in all you can about these titles. Look at their sales rankings. Read their reviews. What do readers like about the books? Dislike? Want more or less of? What do they care about? What are their hot buttons? Study their packaging and marketing. Can you infer the reasoning behind how they're titled, designed, and promoted? Note which books customers

---

[21] Both the 10,000 and 80,000 numbers now include some amount of hybrid publishers.

[22] I use micro-publishers to refer to the smallest of publishing companies—those with just 1–3 employees, releasing 1–3 titles a year, and probably with annual revenues well under $500,000. Sometimes these are the publishing arm of a nonprofit, school, church, historical society, or professional organization. It should not be assumed that a micro-publisher puts out a lesser quality of book or is lacking a proper publishing infrastructure to adequately release your book into the world, but the due diligence is on you.

also purchased. Finally, you want to know…who is publishing books such as yours?

Keep your notes here about the titles, but start your master list of publishers elsewhere. You'll need lots of room.

_____

_____

_____

_____

_____

_____

_____

_____

_____

_____

_____

_____

_____

_____

_____

_____

_____

_____

☐ Visit the biggest bookseller near you, and see which companies are publishing books on your topic and closely-related topics. Note those publishers whose approach, style, design, vibe, etc. you like and are a good fit for your book and its intended audience. Where Amazon can give you breadth, depth, and near-instant information, there is also much to be gleaned from holding physical books and assessing their properties and the decision-making that went into them.

What have you noticed about the relevant books you've found?

_____
_____
_____
_____
_____
_____
_____
_____
_____
_____
_____
_____
_____

Which publishers should top your list?

_____
_____
_____
_____
_____
_____
_____
_____
_____
_____
_____
_____
_____
_____
_____

☐ As you go about the above two activities, create a list of desirable and suitable publishers. Aim for a list of at least 50 to 100 publishers—seriously. Consider any press that might be a match: micro, small, independent, niche, regional, academic, nonprofit, organizational, and religious.

Quantity is important! Set a goal for when you will finish this list, and take note of anything you need to remember to make it happen.

_____

_____

_____

_____

_____

_____

_____

_____

_____

_____

_____

_____

☐ Consult the *Literary Marketplace* guide found in the reference section of most libraries to see which publishers are looking for books on your topic. This hefty annual contains detailed entries on publishers that include such information as publishing specialties, submission policies, acquisitions practices, etc., along with useful articles for aspiring authors. Add the most interesting and relevant publishers to the list you've started. (LMP is available online for subscribers. If you're feeling spendy, the annual fee is $400, but $25 for a week's access serves just as well for the diligent and organized.)

When will you go to the library or spend time online?

_____

_____

☐ There are various other directories and listings of publishers online, but in my experience, they are mostly redundant (if you've done the above steps) and/or heavy on teeny-tiny, out-of-business, scamming, or self-publishing (pay-to-play) operations.

☐ Visit the websites of companies on your list, and spend time getting a sense of who they are.

Schedule this on your calendar.

☐ While on those websites, read the company's submission guidelines (nearly 100% of publishers' websites now contain this information, and you usually don't have to dig around too much for it either). If you learn your book is not a good fit for them, remove them from your list and move on.

After you've visited a number of them, have you learned anything new about book publishing that you'd like to keep in mind?

_____

_____

_____

_____

_____

_____

_____

_____

_____

_____

_____

☐ As you go, prioritize your list of potential publishers based on a combination of your book's right fit for them and their desirability for you. (To expand your idea of what *you* might want to get out of publishing your book, see the **Master Checklist of the Benefits of Being an Author** at the end of this book.)

After reviewing the Benefits of Being an Author checklist, which benefits stand out for you?

_____

_____

_____

_____

_____

_____

_____

_____

_____

_____

_____

_____

_____

_____

☐ Next, submit your book proposal package per the website instructions (to a tee) to the publishers on your list, starting at the top and working down. (Think big from the start. Don't "work up" to them!) Simultaneous submissions are okay unless stated otherwise. Divide up the work as makes sense to you, but I'd advise sending them out in batches of 2 to 10 each day in a steady stream until you either reach the end or have a contract. Commit to the project, and concentrate your efforts. Don't drag it out. Publishing takes a long time! You either want to find a publisher in a reasonable amount of time or move on to considering self-publishing or hybrid options.

At what rate will you be sending out your pitches? What time each day? What will you have to do to keep that time reserved for pitches?

_____

_____

_____

_____

_____

_____

_____

_____

_____

_____

☐ If a publisher's submission guidelines aren't specific, keep in mind the information in this workbook and create a package most likely to persuade them. Think of it as a "business plan" for your book and a "business agreement" between you and the publisher, and it will be hard to go wrong.

Notes on the business plan for your book and the desired business agreement with a publisher:

_____

_____

_____

_____

_____

_____

_____

_____

_____

_____

☐ Keeping in mind the restrictions the publisher lets you know about in advance, the publishing process *from the publisher's perspective*, and the items outlined on the included checklists, give them your best, savviest shot. Know that you are essentially competing—even at the smallest presses—against hundreds or thousands of others for only a few coveted spots. Use your passion and imagination to catch their attention, pique their interest, impress them, and persuade them. Do whatever won't cause them to immediately know your proposal's a "no."

Is there anything you especially want to keep in mind about the publisher's perspective?

_____

_____

_____

_____

_____

_____

_____

_____

_____

☐ Unless the submission guidelines prohibit it (or politely request not to do it), plan to check in with every publisher you've contacted and not heard back from 30–45 days after your initial contact.

Add these checking-back tasks to your calendar or to-do list now.

☐ Use *every* aspect of your initial contact(s) with a publisher to show your professionalism, your attention to detail, your work ethic, and your understanding of their business and their point of view. All other things being equal, they'll almost always choose the author who's more professional and easier to work with.

☐ If anyone takes the time to send you a few notes about your book (with their rejection), see what you can learn from the experience and take steps to use that knowledge to your benefit. Tweak future submissions as necessary.

What sort of feedback are you getting? Is it useful? How will you adjust your proposal going forward?

_____
_____
_____
_____
_____
_____
_____
_____
_____

☐ Don't give up. Periodically review your proposal with fresh eyes, and upgrade it as necessary. Get advice from others (preferably those with some knowledge of the process). Keep sending it out. Keep your brain trained on new ways to pitch your book, on new opportunities to get it published, and on ways to improve your book in the meantime.

Keep track of your new ideas as they occur to you.

_____
_____
_____
_____

☐ Create and know your contingency plan. Create a schedule around it. How long will you devote to finding a publisher? If you don't find a publisher in that amount of time, will or won't you pursue self-publishing? What self-publishing options are out there, how and when will you learn about them, and how will you assess them?

Answer the above questions for yourself. Keep in mind the value of what you have to offer, what it is that you want, and that you have choices at every step.

Conclusion

That's it! Congratulations to you for taking this first step to properly inform yourself and orient yourself to the task in front of you. I wish you all the best.

If you have a general question about this process that you don't find answered here, drop me an email and I'll answer it (if I have an answer) for free: sharon@everythinggoesmedia.com.

Sharon

May I help you further? Please visit Conspire Creative (www.conspirecreative.com), my strategic support firm that offers consulting, coaching, editorial, and mediation services to authors, publishers, and content enterprises. You can read testimonials from past clients here: https://www.conspirecreative.com/testimonials

BONUS! Master Checklist of the Benefits of Being an Author

What benefits do *you* want from writing a book? (The more honest you can be with yourself, the better.) Once you have a clear idea of the few or dozens of things you hope to enjoy, gain, and achieve with your book's release into the world, you can start developing a marketing and promotion plan that works towards those things. That will go a long way towards making the months and years of book promotion less about drudgery and disappointment and more about fulfillment, perks, learning new things, and milestones.

In no particular order...

Community/Social Benefits

- ☐ Gaining entry to the "club" of writers.
- ☐ Participating in the community interested in one's topic.
- ☐ Joining the conversations related to one's book/topic.
- ☐ Making a difference in the lives of others.
- ☐ Winning converts to a cause.
- ☐ Popularizing one's ideas.
- ☐ Swaying public opinion.
- ☐ Correcting misconceptions.
- ☐ Exposing injustices.
- ☐ Entertaining and delighting others.
- ☐ Capturing stories before they're lost.
- ☐ Preserving history before it's lost.
- ☐ Bringing attention to local businesses.
- ☐ Meeting interesting, new people.
- ☐ Amplifying one's social network.

Personal/Internal Benefits

- ☐ Expressing oneself.
- ☐ Creating something original, beautiful, provocative, important, and _____ (fill in the blank).
- ☐ Experiencing elevated self-esteem.
- ☐ Enjoying personal satisfaction for having written a book.
- ☐ Achieving something significant.
- ☐ Accomplishing one of the top goals of your fellow human beings, rather than just talking or thinking about doing it.
- ☐ Springboarding to bigger and better things.
- ☐ Opening doors (public speaking, media interviews, and business opportunities).
- ☐ Practicing a hobby more fully.
- ☐ Learning new skills (blogging, public speaking, being media savvy, mastering social media, networking, etc.).
- ☐ Enhancing existing skills (writing, editing, speaking, etc.).
- ☐ Overcoming personal obstacles (procrastination, shyness, etc.).
- ☐ Making a name for oneself.
- ☐ Sharing unique experiences and perspectives.
- ☐ Becoming better-known, well-known, or famous.
- ☐ Basking in the prestige.
- ☐ Living a fuller life.
- ☐ Leaving a legacy.

Career/Business Benefits

- ☐ Establishing one's authority on a subject.
- ☐ Showing expertise in a field.
- ☐ Defining one's position (role) and position (perspective) in some area.
- ☐ Contributing to a body of knowledge.
- ☐ Boosting one's reputation.
- ☐ Exhibiting leadership.
- ☐ Leveraging the power of the printed word.
- ☐ Complementing one's primary business.
- ☐ Advancing in one's field.

☐ Enlarging one's professional network.
☐ Having something to give away (a calling card, gift, or premium).
☐ Developing a side business.
☐ Building a "platform" (growing an ongoing audience).

Financial Benefits

☐ Earning passive income[23] (royalties).
☐ Increasing income through turning one's book into a cottage industry[24] (re-selling, speaking fees, etc.).
☐ Reaping the rewards of the content's secondary markets (movie rights, reprint rights, etc.).
☐ Finding a better-paying job (with new skills and an enhanced resumé).
☐ Justifying a pay raise (increased value to one's company).
☐ Extending the reach of one's business (passively locating new customers).

---

[23] It's only "passive" income after you've done loads of unpaid work first, amiright?
[24] A home-based, creative, and/or small-scale side hustle, enterprise, business.

About the Author

Sharon Woodhouse is the owner of Everything Goes Media (www.everythinggoesmedia.com), a publishing company with 4 imprints and a consulting division, Conspire Creative (www.conspirecreative.com). She started her independent press nearly 25 years ago, expanded it to include consulting for authors and publishers 10–15 years ago, and added coaching for authors and publishers, project management, print brokering, mediations, and hybrid publishing in the last 5 years. She has seen and done most things in the small press world and works daily on the front lines of the business trying to stay one step ahead of the game!

Woodhouse's businesses and the authors and books she has published have been featured in hundreds of local, national, and international media outlets, including A&E, the BBC, *Business Week*, the *Chicago Sun-Times*, the *Chicago Tribune*, CNN, *Crain's Chicago Business*, FOX, the History Channel, National Public Radio, the National Geographic Channel, the *New York Times*, the Travel Channel, *USA Today*, the *Wall Street Journal*, the *Washington Post*, and WGN-TV.

Woodhouse has taken an entrepreneurial approach to just about everything since first becoming self-employed as a teenager 3 decades ago. She has directly counseled and coached hundreds of small business owners, solo professionals, creatives, authors, publishers, and job-changers. Sharon received her coaching training from Coach Training Alliance and is a certified professional coach and a member of the International Coach Federation. She is the author of *The Coach Within: 28 Big Ideas to Engage the Power of Your Own Wisdom, Creativity, and Choices*.

Amazon Reviews

Do you have an opinion about or endorsement of what you've read here? Please leave a review for *Pitch What's True* at Amazon.com, LibraryThing.com, and/or Goodreads.com.

Future Books and Classes

If you would like to be informed about future publishing titles and classes from author, coach, and publisher Sharon Woodhouse, please email conspirecreative@everythinggoesmedia.com to be added to the list.

Coaching

Sharon Woodhouse makes business, personal, and "philosophy of life" coaching accessible to all coachable individuals with sliding-scale rates (www.conspirecreative.com/coaching). Contact her at sharon@everythinggoesmedia.com for more information and to set up a free consult.